SHOCK ZONE™
GAMES AND GAMERS

THE EPIC EVOLUTION OF VIDEO GAMES

PORTER COUNTY PUBLIC LIBRARY

ARIE KAPLAN

Lerner Publications Company • Minneapolis

NOTE TO READERS: Not all games are appropriate for
players of all ages. Remember to follow video game
rating systems and the advice of a parent or guardian
when deciding which games to play.

Lerner Publications Company
A division of Lerner Publishing Group, Inc.
241 First Avenue North
Minneapolis, MN 55401 U.S.A.

Website address: www.lernerbooks.com

Content Consultant: Crystle Martin, postdoctoral researcher, Digital
Media and Learning Hub at the University of California, Irvine

Library of Congress Cataloging-in-Publication Data
Kaplan, Arie.
    The epic evolution of video games / by Arie Kaplan.
        pages cm. — (Shockzone—games and gamers)
    Includes index.
    ISBN 978-1-4677-1248-4 (lib. bdg. : alk. paper)
    ISBN 978-1-4677-1783-0 (eBook)
    1. Video games—History—Juvenile literature. I. Title.
  GV1469.3.K36 2014
  794.809—dc23   2012048032

Manufactured in the United States of America
1 — MG — 7/15/13

TABLE OF CONTENTS

THE FIRST VIDEO GAMES

Chances are you have a favorite video game, whether it's *Call of Duty, Angry Birds, Super Mario Bros.,* or *Madden NFL*. That's no surprise. **Video games are a huge part of our culture.**

But it wasn't always like this. Ever wonder what the first games were? Or how gaming became such a big deal? Read on to find out.

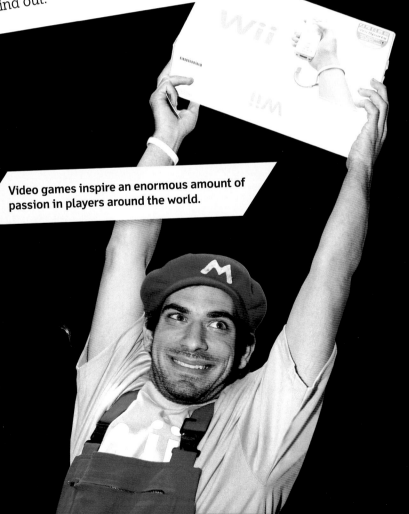

Video games inspire an enormous amount of passion in players around the world.

If you went back in time to the 1950s and told someone that video games would one day fit in your hand, they would've laughed in your face. Computers took up whole rooms in university laboratories. Only scientists could make and play games.

But don't feel too disappointed. The games were terrible. In one game, *Bouncing Ball*, a dot appeared at the top of the screen, fell to the bottom, and rolled away. Yep, you read right. That was the whole game. Boring!

In 1966 an engineer invented the first video game console that could be hooked up to TV sets. It was nicknamed the Brown Box. Despite the lame name, it amazed the people who saw it. The electronics company Magnavox smartly renamed it the Odyssey and released it in 1972. Within a few years, video games were a national sensation.

Computers fit in the palm of your hand now, but in the 1960s, they were gigantic.

THE GOLDEN AGE

If you tried to think up a great new video game character today, chances are you wouldn't think of a big, angry gorilla, a leaping carpenter, or a yellow circle. But those weird ideas became some of the most famous game characters of the 1970s and the 1980s. This time became known as the Golden Age of video games. There was an explosion of new kinds of games and consoles.

The company Atari released its Atari 2600 console in 1977. People could play hundreds of different games on the same console. All they had to do was plug in different cartridges.

cartridges =
plastic devices
containing computer
chips that store
video games in their
memory

One of the first popular game characters was Pac-Man, a yellow circular creature. His game, *Pac-Man*, came out in 1980. In the game, Pac-Man ran through a maze and escaped from colorful ghosts. Along the way, he munched on white dots called power pellets. Occasionally he'd gulp down fruit for extra bonus points. Strange idea for a game, don't you think? But *Pac-Man* quickly became the hottest game in America.

Pac-Man was so popular it inspired a hit 1982 song called "Pac-Man Fever."

Donkey Kong was another hit from the Golden Age. Nintendo released it in 1981. The game involved two important characters. The first was a big, angry gorilla with the bizarre name Donkey Kong. The second was a carpenter named Jumpman. *Donkey Kong* was a platformer game, meaning that the player had to run and jump across platforms. In this case, the player guided Jumpman across these platforms to rescue a woman named Lady from Donkey Kong's clutches. Clearly, early video game creators had some weird ideas about naming things.

Nintendo later changed Jumpman's job from carpenter to plumber and renamed him Mario. He became one of the most famous characters in video game history.

DONKEY KONG

Many people wonder how Donkey Kong got his name. The game's Japanese creator, Shigeru Miyamoto, spoke little English. He wanted to call the gorilla "Stubborn Gorilla." He looked through a Japanese-English dictionary to find synonyms for these words. *Donkey* was listed as a synonym for stubborn. *Kong* (as in King Kong) was listed as a synonym for gorilla.

THE CRASH

In the world of business, a crash occurs when an industry collapses. The video game industry suffered a devastating crash in 1983. There were several reasons for this epic failure.

For one thing, stacks and stacks of low-quality games filled up store shelves. When companies noticed video games were crazy popular, they rushed to sell their own games. They didn't care if the games were total garbage. They just wanted to make tons of cash super quickly. Not surprisingly, the quality of games took a nosedive.

One hilariously tragic example of these awful games is *E.T. The Extra-Terrestrial*. It came out for the Atari 2600 in 1982 and was based on the popular movie of the same name. Usually, large

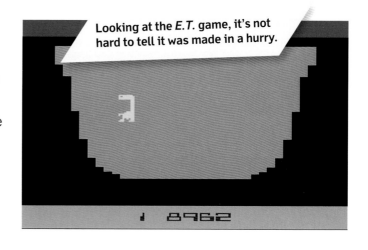

Looking at the *E.T.* game, it's not hard to tell it was made in a hurry.

companies spend at least six months to make a video game. But with *E.T.*, Atari told one guy to make it from scratch in just six weeks. In the game, players had to find pieces of a phone so the main character could call his home planet. Yawn.

The game was a gigantic disaster for Atari, and word quickly spread about how bad it was. Atari ended up having to bury millions of unsold *E.T.* cartridges in the New Mexico desert.

Another reason for the crash was that too many different consoles were available. If you think the number of video games in stores today is crazy, that's nothing compared to the early 1980s. It became tough for people to even figure out which games went with which consoles. For instance, the Atari 5200 was unable to play Atari 2600 games. Few people cared about the new console, and it was discontinued within two years.

Atari's follow-up to the 2600, the Atari 5200, disappointed consumers and helped lead to the crash.

VIDEO GAMES STRIKE BACK

In the late 1980s, the video game industry came roaring back from the dark days of the crash. It did this by offering gamers **new consoles, new characters, and new genres.**

A huge part of this comeback was one of the most famous consoles of all time, the Nintendo Entertainment System (NES). When Nintendo launched the console in the United States in 1985, it became a smash hit. If you've ever been lucky enough to play one, you'll know why. Even though the graphics were simple, the NES had some of the best games in history.

Two of these games made Nintendo the video game king of the late 1980s. Both were created by Shigeru Miyamoto. The first was a platformer called *Super Mario Bros.*, released in 1985. The main characters were Mario and his brother Luigi. Once again, Nintendo took super-

Shigeru Miyamoto stands in front of his most famous character, Mario.

weird ideas and made them hugely popular. The plumbers Mario and Luigi collected gold coins, mushrooms, and flaming flowers on their way to defeat a spiky-shelled dinosaur. *Mario* was an instant hit.

The second game was *Legend of Zelda*, released in 1987. Compared to the weirdness of *Mario*, *Zelda* seemed downright normal. Players guided the hero Link through forests, caverns, and dungeons. *Zelda* was an open-world game, meaning that players could freely explore the game world rather than following a single path. This type of gameplay can still be seen in modern games such as *Grand Theft Auto IV* and *Skyrim*.

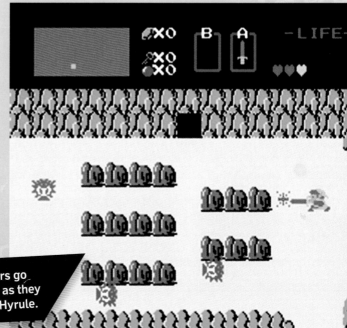

Legend of Zelda let players go anywhere they wanted to as they explored the kingdom of Hyrule.

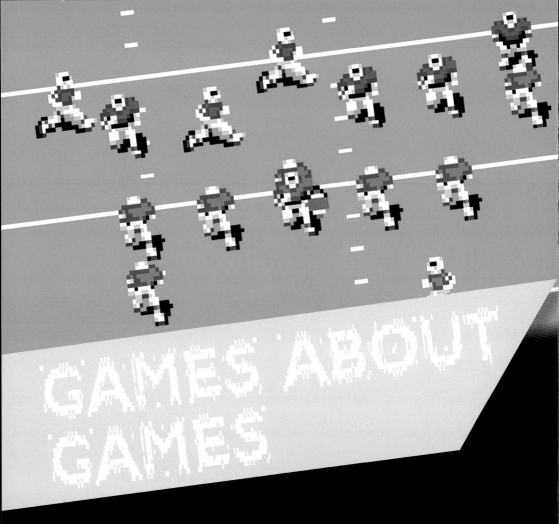

GAMES ABOUT GAMES

If you've ever watched football, you know that a lot of things are going on at the same time. More than twenty players, a moving football, and a huge crowd—there was no way the game consoles of the 1970s could handle all that stuff. But in the late 1980s, game technology began finally catching up. One of the reasons earlier games had been so strange was because they didn't have to show things that existed in real life. Yellow circles chomping on power pellets and jumping cartoon carpenters are one thing. But showing things that real people do—such as sports—is a whole different ball game.

The company Electronic Arts released *John Madden Football* in 1988. *Madden* games still come out every year. Other sports games came before it. But *Madden* was special for several reasons.

First, football coach John Madden was a consultant on the game. This meant that he gave expert advice to the game designers. As a result, *John Madden Football* was more realistic than earlier sports games. The game was one of the first to show complete football teams. Up to twenty-two players appeared on-screen at once.

Of course, the graphics were still nowhere near those used today. Players who were running looked as though they were basically sliding across the field on ice skates. And although weather could be changed in the game, a sunny day looked no different from a raging blizzard.

Sports games still had a long way to go. There were no real team names or player names in *John Madden Football*. The days of true realism were years in the future. But the first *Madden* game raised the bar for sports games and let the consoles of the late 1980s flex their graphical muscles.

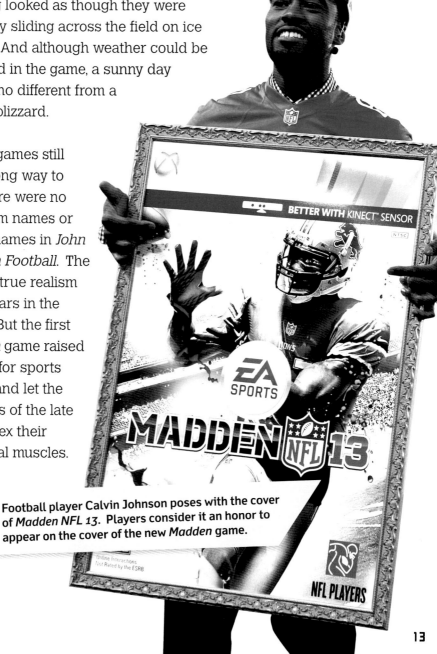

Football player Calvin Johnson poses with the cover of *Madden NFL 13*. Players consider it an honor to appear on the cover of the new *Madden* game.

GAMES TO GO

Until the 1980s, most gamers' backsides were basically glued to their couches. Home video game consoles were the only way to play. But this all changed in 1989 when Nintendo unleashed the handheld game console known as the Game Boy. Rather than being tied to a screen at home, players could now access a screen on the playground, in the car, or at boring relatives' homes.

With the Game Boy, Nintendo singlehandedly kicked off a craze for portable video game consoles and changed the game industry forever. If you play video games, chances are you've played on a handheld. Game Boy was not the first handheld, but it was the first one gamers cared about. Why had it succeeded where others had failed miserably?

First of all, it was much more high-tech than most previous handhelds. Its graphics and sound ran circles around older systems like Milton Bradley's Microvision, released in 1979. It also included a headphone jack. With headphones, gamers could crank up the sound without bothering the people around them.

Another key to the Game Boy's success was the addictive puzzle game *Tetris*. The game came free with every Game Boy sold. The game was basically a geometry nightmare. A never-ending stream of shapes fell from the top of the screen. Players had to fit them together to get rid of them. *Tetris* was simple, but gamers couldn't get enough of it. Some people even reported having dreams about falling shapes.

Other companies released their own handhelds. Unfortunately, they were horrible. The Atari Lynx and the Sega Game Gear were bulkier and more expensive than the Game Boy. They also ate up batteries faster than an elephant eating at a buffet. Both the Lynx and the Game Gear failed miserably. Nintendo went on to sell more than 60 million Game Boys.

Handhelds, including the Nintendo 3DS shown here, are still a big deal in the gaming world.

BIGGER, BETTER, AND FASTER

During the 1990s, game designers used new technology to build on their success. It was obvious that video games were here to stay. Graphics became better, animation became smoother, and stories became more interesting.

A new platformer came out for the Sega Genesis home console in 1991 and became an instant hit. It starred a speedy blue hedgehog named Sonic. Based on this, can you guess what the game was called? Hint: it's exactly what you'd expect. Yep—it was *Sonic the Hedgehog*.

Sonic had some major attitude, especially compared to other video game characters who lacked personality. If the player stopped moving for more than a few moments, Sonic would stare at the screen and tap his foot impatiently. Without actually speaking, he was basically saying, "Hurry up! I want to MOVE!" Sonic's love of speed showed off the power of the Genesis. Sonic sprinted at top speed through colorful levels, ran up walls, and rolled around loops. After *Sonic*, Sega began seeing some success. People loved how quickly the game moved. Soon, gamers were buying the Sega Genesis just to play *Sonic*.

Sega's Genesis was designed to directly compete with Nintendo's NES. In the same way, the character of Sonic competed with Nintendo's Mario. It worked. *Sonic the Hedgehog* made Sega into Nintendo's biggest rival. So, by the early 1990s, the top video game stars on Earth were a blue hedgehog and a pudgy plumber.

Mario has appeared in an amazing number of games—more than two hundred by 2013.

When Satoshi Tajiri was a child growing up in Japan, he liked to wander around the forest outside of town and collect insects. He was interested in the differences between them. You probably wouldn't expect his hobby to lead to video games, movies, TV shows, and billions of dollars.

But Tajiri became a video game designer as an adult, and his childhood hobby resulted in the Game Boy game *Pokémon*, released in 1996. Players caught, collected, and battled monsters of all shapes and sizes. *Pokémon* was an unbelievable success, selling millions of copies.

Pokémon is a role-playing game, or RPG. In an RPG, the player controls and shapes a character that goes on adventures. By beating up on huge hordes of bad guys, he or she gains money, supplies, and skills. The RPG genre got its start in the 1980s.

Shortly after *Pokémon* came out, a new computer game brought big changes for RPGs. The game was *Ultima Online*. It was a type of RPG called a MMORPG. Okay, let's break down that bowl of alphabet soup. The letters stand for: massively multiplayer online role-playing game. These games take place in worlds that exist on the Internet rather than on one person's console. Millions of players can play together at the same time. The success of *Ultima Online* led to popular MMORPGs like *Everquest* and *World of Warcraft*.

ONLINE SAFETY

Many recent games allow players to communicate with one another online. Because of this, it is necessary to be careful. Never give anyone your personal information. The people you're communicating with might not be who they say they are.

More than 10 million people play *World of Warcraft*.

GAMES GET REAL

In the new millennium, game designers took the quality of game graphics and sound to the next level. New games created simulations that blurred the line between games and real life. Now, the only limit was the imagination of the game designer.

simulation = a genre of game in which players act out real-world situations or events

With this amazing gaming power in mind, if you had the chance to design your own video game, what would your characters do? Would they do everyday tasks like get jobs, build homes, and raise families? Maybe that sounds kinda boring. But that's exactly what game designer Will Wright did in 2000 when he created *The Sims*. Many other games took place in unrealistic fantasy worlds. But the everyday situations in *The Sims* proved irresistible to millions of players. By 2002 *The Sims* had become the best-selling PC game ever.

The Sims was part of the genre known as casual games. In casual games, there are simple controls, little story, and no ultimate goal. Players can pick it up and play it for a short time without worrying about getting to new levels or beating the game.

Another breakthrough came in 2001 with the release of *Halo: Combat Evolved* on Microsoft's Xbox console. The game was an FPS, or a first-person shooter. In this type of game, the player sees through the eyes of the character. *Halo*'s detailed science-fiction world contained frightening aliens, enormous spaceships, and huge battles. But the game also presented an interesting story and characters that players cared about.

Master Chief is the star of the *Halo* games.

OUT OF CONTROL

If you thought the only way to play video games was with buttons and joysticks, you'd be totally wrong. Things used to be that way, but it all changed in 2005 with the release of *Guitar Hero*. It first came out for Sony's PlayStation 2 console. In the game, players used a plastic guitar-shaped controller to transform themselves into radical virtual rock stars.

Like *The Sims*, *Guitar Hero* turned a normal activity into an exciting gaming experience. There were no quests, zombies, or superheroes. Players just rocked out with their friends.

Nintendo introduced an even cooler way to control games in 2006 as part of its Wii console. With the Wii, Nintendo turned motion controls into a worldwide sensation. The Wii controller looked like a TV remote. Moving it around in real life moved things on-screen. In a baseball game, you could swing it like a bat. In bowling you held the remote as you pretend to roll a bowling ball. It was ridiculously simple, yet it was a giant hit. Many people who didn't usually play games now enjoyed them.

The Wii changed the way people think about video games. Many players disliked complicated video games involving violence and fast action. Now they enjoyed playing baseball or bowling on the Wii. The console was designed for players of all ages. Many families enjoyed playing it together.

People who didn't normally play video games loved playing the Wii.

CASUAL TAKEOVER

The Finnish game company Rovio released *Angry Birds* for smartphones in 2009. It was a simple puzzle game. These birds were angry for a pretty good reason—a bunch of green pigs stole their eggs. The birds' solution is simple: smash the pigs, knock them over, and basically mess them up. You help them get their revenge by using a slingshot to launch the birds at the pigs. The game became insanely popular. The *Angry Birds* series has been downloaded more than 1 billion times. How did a simple game become such a phenomenon?

Angry Birds soda is just one of many products featuring the furious flyers.

Like *The Sims*, *Angry Birds* was a casual game. Because it was so easy to play, people who didn't usually play games got hooked on it. Also, the game cost just ninety-nine cents. New games for consoles were usually a whopping sixty bucks. Most people could probably find ninety-nine cents in their couch cushions. Players were happy to spend the small sum.

Once fans were addicted, the creators of *Angry Birds* made sequels. They also released the game on computers, home consoles, and handhelds. The *Angry Birds* characters appeared on toys, lunch boxes, and T-shirts. Remember the *Pokémon* craze? Consider this *Pokémon*: Part 2. The success of *Angry Birds* showed how casual gaming has become an enormous part of today's game industry.

The *Angry Birds* characters soon were turned into merchandise of all kinds.

GAME OVER

There's no way to predict what games will be like in the future. Imagine you are standing around talking to gamers forty years ago, making predictions about games today. Could anyone possibly have guessed that graphics would become as crystal clear as Hollywood movies? Or that video games thousands of times more powerful than the top consoles of the 1970s would fit into a pocket or even into a phone? Would they believe that motion controls would let future gamers go bowling, become a rock star, or play tennis in their living rooms? No way.

Trying to imagine video games forty years from now is just as tough. But people are still making guesses. Some people think that we'll eventually control games using only our brains. That's right— mind control. It's not as crazy as it sounds. Even today, scientists are working on artificial arms for amputees that can be controlled with the brain. There's no reason this amazing technology can't be used in the PlayStation 17.

The way we see games might also be due for a big change. Since the 1970s, we've played games on televisions. Some people think that we may someday play within virtual reality, wearing headsets so that the game world is visible all around us. Imagine playing a *Halo* game where you can simply turn your head to follow a spaceship as it crashes and burns across the sky of an alien world. Pretty cool, right?

Game developers are still figuring out what video games can be and do. Games have already moved from computer labs to living rooms to the palms of players' hands. Where will they be tomorrow? Will new technologies change the way we play? How can the player be more fully absorbed in the world of a video game? And how will he or she control it? There's no telling what new thrills and challenges the future of gaming might bring!

Can you tell whether this is a photo or a video game screenshot? In the future, it will be even tougher to tell the difference.

1. *Call of Duty: Black Ops II* (Xbox 360, PS3, Wii U) (*right*)
This game is the latest in the best-selling *Call of Duty* first-person shooter series. It is the sequel to 2010's *Call of Duty: Black Ops*. (*Call of Duty* is rated M for Mature.)

2. *Madden NFL 13* (Xbox 360, PS3, Wii U) (*left*)
Each year, the latest *Madden* game always finds its way to the best-seller list. The newest version of the game features an advanced animation system.

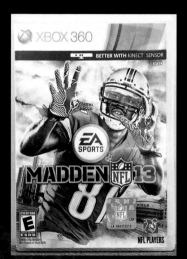

3. *Halo 4* (Xbox 360)
Fans of the *Halo* series had been waiting five years for a true sequel to 2007's *Halo 3*. For millions of players, the latest *Halo* game was definitely worth the wait. (*Halo 4* is rated M for Mature.)

4. *Assassin's Creed III* (Xbox 360, PS3, Wii U)
In the *Assassin's Creed* games, players take on the role of an assassin. (Duh). The third game puts players square in the middle of the American Revolution. (*Assassin's Creed III* is rated M for Mature.)

5. *Just Dance 4* (Xbox 360, PS3, Wii U)
In this dancing game, players use motion controllers to follow the moves of dancers on the screen.

6. *NBA 2K13* (Xbox 360, PS3, Wii U)
Rapper Jay-Z helped create the latest edition of the top video game basketball series.

7. *Borderlands 2* (Xbox 360, PS3)
(*right*)
Borderlands features a unique cartoony style of graphics and a huge assortment of weapons. Millions of gamers love the combination. (*Borderlands 2* is rated M for Mature.)

8. *Call of Duty: Modern Warfare 3* (Xbox 360, PS3, Wii)
The *Call of Duty* series is so popular that last year's version often ends up on the current top-seller list. (*Call of Duty* is rated M for Mature.)

9. *Lego Batman 2: DC Super Heroes* (Xbox 360, PS3, Wii) (*left*)
This game combines the popular Lego toys with famous comic book characters.

10. *FIFA Soccer 13* (Xbox 360, PS3, Wii)
FIFA Soccer 13 is the latest soccer game in a series that dates back to 1993.

FURTHER INFORMATION

Bissell, Tom. *Extra Lives: Why Video Games Matter.* New York: Vintage Books, 2011.
Fifty years ago, the video game industry didn't exist. Today it rakes in about $80 billion a year. In this book, journalist Tom Bissell explores why this happened and what it all means.

Dillon, Roberto. *The Golden Age of Video Games: The Birth of a Multibillion Dollar Industry.* Boca Raton, FL: A K Peters, 2011.
If you want to learn more about the Golden Age of games, look no further than this book. It also includes screenshots of some of the best games, as well as a handy timeline.

IGN
http://www.ign.com
This website is one of today's biggest sources for video game news and reviews. The best part? Their reviews go back more than fifteen years, making the site a great place to learn about older classic games.

Kohler, Chris. *Power-Up: How Japanese Video Games Gave the World an Extra Life.* Indianapolis: BradyGames, 2004.
Most of the major game companies of today—Nintendo, Sega, and Sony—began in Japan. This book takes a look at how games from Japan reached worldwide popularity.

Loguidice, Bill, and Matt Barton. *Vintage Games: An Insider Look at the History of Grand Theft Auto, Super Mario, and the Most Influential Games of All Time.* Oxford: Focal Press, 2009.
This book takes in-depth looks at some of the most important games in video game history. It includes chapters on *John Madden Football*, *The Sims*, and *Pac-Man*.

Melissinos, Chris, and Patrick O'Rourke. *The Art of Video Games: From Pac-Man to Mass Effect.* New York: Welcome Books, 2012.
In 2012 one of America's biggest art museums featured a display on the art of video games. This book includes a huge collection of images from that exhibit.

Ryan, Jeff. *Super Mario: How Nintendo Conquered America.* New York: Portfolio, 2011.
Did you know Nintendo originally started off as a playing card company? Learn this and other cool facts in this history of the company.

LERNER

SOURCE

Expand learning beyond the printed book. Download free, complementary educational resources for this book from our website, www.lerneresource.com.

PHOTO ACKNOWLEDGMENTS

The images in this book are used with the permission of: © Jeff Lewis/AP Images, p. 4; © Aerojet-General/W.E. Miller/AP Images, p. 5; © Nick Ut/AP Images, p. 6; © AP Images, p. 7; © Bettmann/Corbis/AP Images, p. 8; © Red Line Editorial, pp. 9 (top), 11 (bottom), 12, 28 (bottom); © Evan Amos, pp. 9 (bottom), 10; © Paul Sakuma/AP Images, pp. 11 (top), 20; © Ed Rieker/AP Images for National Football League, p. 13; © William Warby, p. 14; © Kyodo/AP Images, p. 15; © Lev Radin/Shutterstock Images, p. 16; © PRNewsFoto/Nintendo/AP Images, p. 17; © John T. Barr, Nintendo/AP Images, p. 18; © Blizzard/dapd/AP Images, p. 19; © Microsoft/dapd/AP Images, p. 21; © Hillsdale Daily News, Pete Mowry/AP Images, p. 22; © Shizuo Kambayashi/ AP Images, p. 23 (top); © Diane Bondareff/PRNewsFoto/Nintendo, p. 23 (bottom); © manley099/iStockphoto, p. 24; © robtek/iStockphoto, p. 25 (top); © Ziva_K/ iStockphoto, p. 25 (bottom); © Barone Firenze/Shutterstock Images, p. 26; © PRNewsPhoto/Mercedes-Benz USA/AP Images, p. 27; © shaunl/iStockphoto, p. 28 (top); © 2K Games/AP Images, p. 29 (top); © Warner Bros./AP Images, p. 29 (bottom).

Front cover: © INTERFOTO/Alamy (top); © Pixellover RM 8/Alamy (bottom).

Main body text set in Calvert MT Std Regular 11/16.
Typeface provided by Monotype Typography.